"PARENTS

LIKE

ME"

PARENTS

LIKE

ME

As we all have felt that we are alone. This book is a reminder that we are not. As we are anointed to become parents, we can all relate to some if not all what others have experienced. I pray that as you are looking for some solutions, that you find what you seek as well as encourage you to create some tactics of your own!

Stay encouraged as we attempt to become the parent that our Heavenly Father has been to us.

Felicia McCardy

For more information, please contact

Angel Fergusons' WordProcessing.

Author Felicia McCardy

Publisher Angel Ferguson's WordProcessing 33617

Artwork James Ferguson III

Library of Congress Cataloging –n– Publication Data

Printed in the United States

Ordering sales. Special discounts are available on quantity purchases by corporations, associations and others.

For details, contact the publisher at the address below, Orders by U.S. trade bookstores and wholesalers.

ANGELFERGUSONSWORDPPROCESSING.COM

TEL. 813.516.4916

I'm dedicating this book to my dear mother who passed away Feb 1988. She is the one who I gained strength from before I discovered who God really was. My mother would do what ever she had to do for our family , even working numerous jobs to make sure we never went without. I'm grateful she had the opportunity to meet Keishawn, her first grand child and the only one she would have the pleasure to meet. I'm also dedicating this book to all mother's, father's, sister's, brothers and all family members who make the lives of their special person's life complete.

Hello my name is Felicia McCardy, I would like to share my life with you as a parent of a child with CP. The name Parents Like Me was established as an idea to start a support group for other parents, friend & caregivers that have found themselves looking for ways to handle our lives while taking care of a loved one with CP and other disabilities.

I recently sat down with my publicist to help others to better understand how and why I have taken on the role as caregiver for my daughter Keishawn. One thing is for sure there is no real routine to our routine. What we try to do is make & keep to a schedule when it comes to meal time, bath and bed time. Within these pages, I will share some of the tactics that have been used over the years, one thing is for sure, what may have worked today may not work a week from now.

It is my prayer that you find the words within helpful as well as keeping us and others in your prayers as we will do the same for you.

Felicia McCardy

A mother's love is unconditional

Our days are not perfect but there was never a promise that they would be. Taking care of my daughter has given me an profound respect for those in the medical field. So the next time, you feel that you are all alone and are over whelmed, please remember that you are not. Become rest assured that God will send that special someone to become that ear when you need to talk, that shoulder you need when you become tiresome and that voice when you need to hear a joke so that you may laugh away the stress.

Good morning I say to myself. Not knowing what this day may bring.

As I listen to her crying out I say "why" and yet at the same time I am wondering what is wrong with my daughter now? I often think of myself as well as others who have a voice, a good mind and yet no one can hear them. There are times that I wish she could speak about the things she would like, the things that she needs.

As well as the things that are causing her pain. But it is said that we were all created equal in God's eyes. So then there is the question, if we were all created equal then why does it appear we all respond to things so differently?

We all know that it takes patience to be a parent. Yet it takes a whole lot more when you are caring for a child with a disability. To tell the truth, it takes patience for all things. But for me it is my faith. It's my trust in God that helps me to get through each day.

I find that the way to get through the day is to encourage myself. I encourage myself to not become tired wiry because there is a life depending on me to feed and bath them as well as support them in all aspects of life.

I can think back when I would sit down ask WHY! WHY ME!

Finally one day I said why not me! Sometimes I look at my friends and family as I say to myself " really, if you had to endure what I went through last night, you would never want to complain again."

I have learned to approach each day as a new beginning, expecting the best. Yes, patiently waiting for God to give me an answer on what to do next.

When caring for someone with a disability there are times that you must pause for some much needed rest. You will find that you are always searching quietly for the right answer. Even when I don't understand I still put my best face and appearance forward. I often think that there is someone standing in the shadows, watching me. For all I know, they could feel that if she can do it, then so can I.

Even in the midst of your ups and downs, keep the faith and simply believe. Believe that there are better days and times ahead.

Take a deep breath and tell yourself, we can do this.

We wanted to do something different with this book. My publicist has decided to have an interview with me to better understand the purpose behind ' Parents Like Me"

On the following pages is a portion of that interview, if you would like to receive a audio version of this interview in it's entirety,

please contact:

ANGELFERGUSONSWORDPROCESSING.COM

Question. Tell me about how your mornings begin.

Response. Our morning begins with breakfast.

Question. How do you prepare her to eat. Is her meal time with the family or is there a time set aside just for her?

Response. On a day to day basis, I feed Kieshawn before the family. This is done to maintain a routine. We make an effort to have dinner together during the holidays and special occasions. Currently she is on mechanically soft foods due to not being able to digest certain particles or forgetting to chew. There are times that I must stimulate her to do so as well as swallow. For instance, spaghetti is easily digested. For the most part, her foods are blended, waffles, pancakes and other soft foods are cut into very small bite sized pieces. Due to some motor skills, I do however will feed her. To put it mildly, everyday is a new day.

Question. Tell me, about the day that your lives changed.

Response. I can remember the day like it was just yesterday, Dec 18, 2003. Although Keishawn had been born with CP, she was a very well functioning in high school. On this particular day, there was a car accident. When she was released from the hospital, it was as if I was bringing home a new born baby. All of progress that had been made was lost. We had begun new long journey. This new journey was not just new to us, but new to her as well. Her world had taken another turn. One that non of us could grasp or understand. But, as a mother I am thankful that she is alive and that God has given me the strength to become her caregiver.

Question. I understand that you are currently at home and not working. Tell me, does Keishawn realize that you are there a lot more?

Response. Yes and no. I say this because my working schedule was always planned around her sleeping schedule. You see, I would work overnight and would return home just in time for her to wake up the next morning.

Question. Tell me about some of things that help to sooth her.

Response. My daughter loves music. She really enjoys gospel music. There are times that she will have at least 3 cd's in the player at one time. Another thing that will sooth her is ice water.. One day I was home with the flu and no one else was there with me and she became agitated. Being weak in bed, I had to think quickly of a way to get her attention so that I could calm her down.. The only thing around me was a glass of ice water. Yes, in trial and error, I took a chance and did a light sprinkle in her face. To my surprise she stopped, calmed down and smiled. This has been one of my methods that I use from time to time. The correct medical term is melt downs, each melt down is trial and error, the key is to find what works.

Question. Is there a period of time that Keishawn is unaware of her surroundings? Does she recognize you as her mother along with other family members?

Response. There are times that she does not recognize us or our home. She will ask for her mother or that she would like to go home. What I have noticed is that this happens in the mornings when she is just waking up. It takes a while to get back into focus. The most important thing is to keep things familiar and not to make drastic changes without treating them as great events. We make an effort to introduce her to change rather than place in an unfamiliar surrounding.

Question. Take me through your routine for bedtime.

Response. Everything is prepared in advance. You must remember, it is like taking care of an infant. There is no time to stop and go grab something. All things must be in arms length.

Once we are in the bathroom, there is a shower chair for her to sit on. Although she is strong in strength she has grown frail in weight. To help her feel secure during the night we have placed bumpers around her bed because she will attempt to roll out of the bed. There are a lot of pillows & padding in her bedroom because she likes to punch the walls. For some reason, she likes the sound of the rhythm of punching. I have learned to make it game and will throw the pillows wherever she decides to throw her next punch.

Question. Does Keishawn enjoy the outdoors?

Response. Yes. We now have a latch and a bell on the doors so that we can hear if she decides to just wonder outside. Once outside, she will stand next to the car, that's her way of telling us she would like to go for a ride.

Question. How does she handle having company at in the home or by meeting new people?

Response. I try and prepare her for visitors by saying "guess who is coming over" as if it is a special occasion just for her. She is usually ok with those that she is familiar with. We currently have a very close knit of family and friends that are aware of Keishawn and the challenges she has. If at any time she becomes agitated, has an outburst or a melt down, they know how to handle themselves and her. It's important to have this type of support with those that we allow in our lives.

Having a daughter with disabilities can have it's challenges. At one time we could go on unplanned trips to see family members that are out of town or just on a family vacation, now those days are just a sweet memory I can recall my passion for fishing, I appreciate those memories yet each day with my daughter out weighs them all.

During this journey of being the caregiver of my daughter there is so much to learn and contain. Knowing what to do and what not to do is not something one can easily pinpoint.

Without caution anything can send her into a series of screaming. I can recall her love for attending to church. This is one place that would always hold her attention. Then all of a sudden she no longer wanted to sit through a service. I had to think really fast on how to hold onto one of things that gives me strength to make it through the day. I remembered her love for babies. So I came up with the idea too keep a baby doll in the car each Sunday. So, once she became agitated in church, I would say " I think the baby came to church today", and I would go out to the car and get the doll for her to hold. For the longest time, no one in the church knew it was a doll. At the time of this publication, we have only attended services this year. Time to find something else that will sooth her. One of the things that we have and will continue to try is introduce her to new restaurants as well re-visit some from the past. I try and select the ones with a calm atmosphere.

Another one of my tactics when Keishawn could not find comfort in sleeping on her bed was to set up my car as a camping trip. Yes, you read that correctly. When making the most of our children's lives we will find ourselves trying some of the most unusual things, but if it works, then it works. Here is what I would do, I would take sheets and put them up to the windows, place pillows on the seat of the car, lock the doors and play music. Amazingly, this is something that really relaxed her. There are times that I've had to drive around at night until her melt down subsided. It is safe to say that no routine is a routine in our day to day lives.

Question. Where is your support system? Are you a part of any support groups? Are there any opportunities for you to have someone to come and sit with her while you have some "me time" so to speak?

Response. My support is my other daughter, Hope. There are those times that she can hear it in my voice or read the expression on my face that I need a break, and she will say, I will take care of Kieshawn for a while. A appreciate all that she has sacrificed throughout the years.

Yet, I apologize for holding her back from pursuing her dreams. I am now encouraging her to live her life, Keishawn is my responsibility. The day, both of them were born, they became my world. I only want the very best for my girls, I am proud of them both. Hope for being so giving, being unselfish of her love and time and for Keishawn for making small steps of progress when others would have given up on her a long time ago. I am often asked, why did I take on this great big role. My reply will always be, why not! God does not place anything upon us that He has not prepared us for. This journey has taught me what it means to love unconditionally. It has taught me how to give mentally and emotionally and no amount of money can replace the two. I feel that I am serving God through being the caregiver of Keishawn, it's so easy to place a disabled child in a group home yet it takes a strong faith to accept the roles of Christ. I want to encourage other parents that through the love of Christ, you can handle this task.

When I am feeling weak, I began to pray. I am thankful that through prayer I am made strong. God gives me the strength to go forward. I say to each of you, I dare you to call on the name of Jesus whether you are dealing with a disabled child or even if you work in the health care field. He will help and guide you through this journey. I encourage you to do something each day for yourself that makes you feel good, even if it doesn't make sense to anyone else.

Here is a guide to help you when you are weak, Phil 4:13, when you are feeling alone you will always have a friend, Hebrews 11:3-5 When you don't understand Psalms 39:1-24. No one said life would be easy when caring for someone with a disability. This life is what you make it.

It is my hope for those that will read this book will find peace and understanding. This life has been given to us for a reason. Find your reason. Never doubt but continue to believe that miracles still happen.

Survival Guide

1. When you are frustrated. Proverbs 21-2

2. When you feel alone. Psalms 23-4

3. When you are simply tired. Psalms 68-35

4. When everything seems to be going wrong. I King 3:3-12

5. When there is no time for you. Proverbs 3:5-6

6. Needing some strength. Isiah 40:29-31

7. When you want to give up. 2 Corinthians 12:9

8. In need of some healing for your heart. 2 Corinthians 12:8-9

9. When you need to feel closer to God. Jeremiah 29:11-13

10. When you feel as if all hope is gone. Jeremiah 29-11

A little about the author Felicia McCardy.

I had strong independent mother who defined being a true mother.

I grew up in Seffner FL.

My first choice of a career was an LPN but I settled for CNA due to being a young mother with Kieshawn. I lost my mother in 1988 lost my sister in 2012 lost a brother in 1992 . When I lost her it hurt really bad but it made me a stronger woman and also just watching her struggle and never giving up. I have 2 daughters, Keishawn 29 and Hope 22 . I named her Hope because I prayed and also hoped thru out my pregnancy she would be normal. I raised my now 24 year old niece since the age of 5 & just recently my then 16 year old niece her sister due to my sister's passing. I LOVE to help others. I use to do a food outreach every Wednesday un I just recently due to a schedule change.

My hobbies, I would say most definitely would be fishing all I need is 1 bite

and I can sit there all day and yes yard sales and flea markets.

My interest would be spending me with family and I love the Lord

he gives me strength from day today.

I don't know where I would be without knowing him!

www.ingramcontent.com/pod-product-compliance
Lightning Source LLC
Chambersburg PA
CBHW060608030426
42337CB00019B/3668